bellicose

flapdoodle

histrion...

TCHOTCHKE

tomfoolery

helter-skelter

contrariwise

PUGILIST

hootenanny

st }...

gadabout

jittery-skittery

CAPRICIOUS

velocipede

imbroglio

{

quixotic

LOLLYGAG

knickerbockers

extravaganza

ne'er-do-well

persnickety

alakazam }

aficionado

COCKAMAMIE

yellow-bellied

peccadillo

BALDERDASH

WISENHEIMER

whippersnapper

scalawag

{ hanker }

fandango

accoutrements

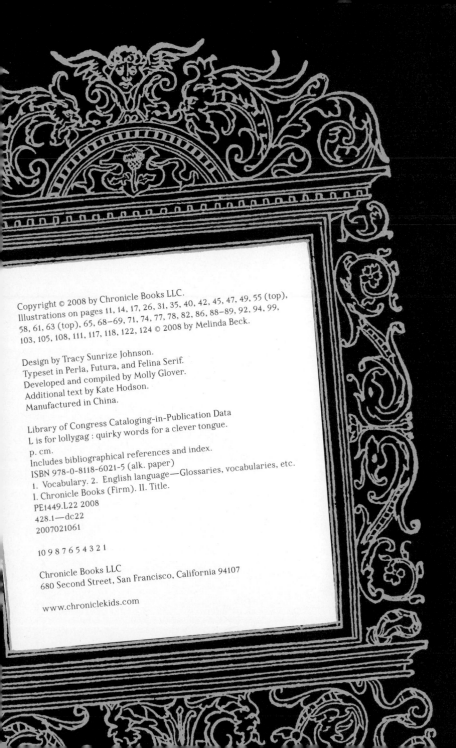

Design by Tracy Sunrize Johnson.
Typeset in Perla, Futura, and Felina Serif.
Developed and compiled by Molly Glover.
Additional text by Kate Hodson.
Manufactured in China.

Library of Congress Cataloging-in-Publication Data
L is for lollygag : quirky words for a clever tongue.
    p. cm.
Includes bibliographical references and index.
ISBN 978-0-8118-6021-5 (alk. paper)
1. Vocabulary. 2. English language—Glossaries, vocabularies, etc.
I. Chronicle Books (Firm). II. Title.
PE1449.L22 2008
428.1—dc22
                                        2007021061

10 9 8 7 6 5 4 3 2 1

Chronicle Books LLC
680 Second Street, San Francisco, California 94107

www.chroniclekids.com

L

Is for

LollyGaG

{ **QUIRKY WORDS** *for a* **CLEVER TONGUE** }

chronicle books · san francisco

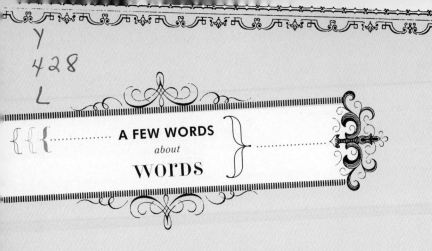

A FEW WORDS
about
WORDS

According to the folks who know these sorts of things, there are about a million words in the English language. But did you know that most English speakers use only a couple thousand of those words in everyday conversation? **Gadzooks!** That means **umpteen** fabulous words are falling by the wayside, unused and forgotten. And when words stop being used, they are in danger of disappearing from our vocabulary altogether.

Of course, making things disappear can be a good thing: A little **"alakazam!"** and there goes that embarrassing photo of you having your diaper changed. But when words are forgotten and disappear, life loses a little **pizzazz**, and our tongues get a little lazier. If we let them, our tongues could get so lazy that they would never again be able to wrap themselves around gems like **carbuncular**, **mollycoddle**, and **flibbertigibbet**.

The good news is you can do your part to stem the tide of lexicon lethargy. With a little **moxie** and a copy of this book, you can become a vocabulary **vigilante**. Think of this book as a source of your secret superpower. In these pages you'll discover (or remember) **oodles** of quirky words that are fun to hear and even more fun to say out loud. Which means if you ever find yourself **hornswoggled** by the neighborhood **rapscallion**, you'll be able to look the **diabolical rogue** squarely in the eye, announce you'll no longer be a victim to his merciless **machinations**, and **swagger** away, leaving him **flummoxed**.

If you don't know any rapscallions, don't worry. Simply knowing and using these words will save them from a **dastardly** fate and will keep your tongue on its toes. Before you know it, you'll find that you can have your **jambalaya** and eat it too. And the world—or at least your corner of it—will be a little less **humbug**, and a little more **hootenanny**.

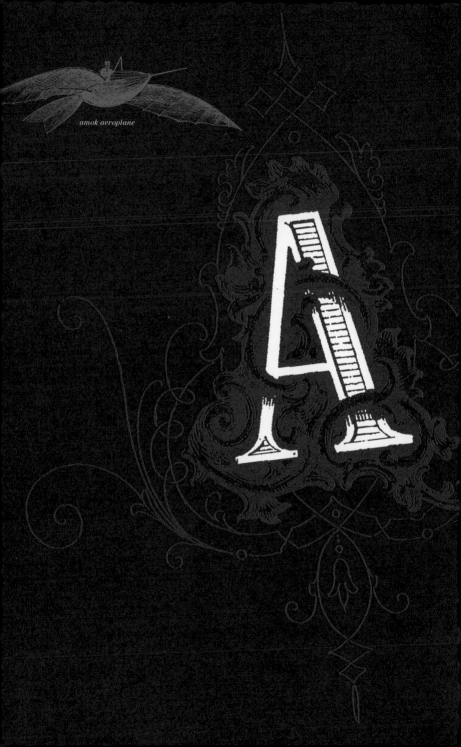

amok aeroplane

abscond (ab-SKOND) *verb*
to disappear suddenly and secretly, usually to avoid getting
in trouble. A person who absconds is an absconder.

accoutrements (uh-KOO-truh-monts) *noun*
accessories or pieces of equipment, like that of a soldier's
uniform; the stuff that makes something what it is (also
known as "characteristics"). If that nursery rhyme is to
be believed, then snips, snails, and puppy dog tails are the
accoutrements of little boys.

aficionado (uh-FISH-ee-uh-NAH-doh) *noun*
someone who is an expert on something, such as geography
or toothpick collecting; if that someone is showing off his or
her expertise, you can say (in a sarcastic way), "Well, aren't
you quite the aficionado!"

agog (uh-GOG) *adjective*
eager or really excited, as in "The students were all agog
watching their teacher get settled in the dunking booth at
the carnival."

AHOY (uh-HOY) *interjection*
another way to say "Hello!" or "Hey there!" It's a standard
greeting of seafaring folk. Alexander Graham Bell was such
a fan of this word that if he'd had his way, "ahoy-hoy" would
be our common telephone greeting today, rather than "hello."

askew alligator

annoyed archer

akimbo (uh-KIM-boh) *adjective, adverb*
standing with your hands on your hips
and your elbows bent outward

alakazam (al-uh-kuh-ZAM) *interjection*
a magical incantation that has a little
more **pizzazz** and oomph than saying
"abracadabra"

alley-oop (al-lee-OOP) *noun, interjection*
Alley Oop is the name of a 1930s comic
strip about a caveman, but an alley-oop
is a basketball maneuver in which one
player throws the ball up toward the
basket and another player jumps up and
dunks the ball into the hoop. It is also
something you can call out when you're
about to do something acrobatic, such as
jumping up and dunking a ball into a hoop.

AMOK (uh-MUK) *adjective, adverb*
going crazy or out of control, like children who've had too
much sugar. People usually run amok because walking amok
would take too long.

askance (uh-SKANS) *adverb*
giving someone a sideways glance or looking at them with
suspicion

askew (uh-SKYOO) *adjective, adverb*
crooked, off-**kilter**, or cockeyed

A
is for

atwitter (uh-TWIH-ter) *adjective*
excited in a nervous-bird kind of a way

awry (uh-RY) *adjective, adverb*
turned around or off course. According to a well-known
proverb, "The best-laid plans of mice and men often go
awry." See also **wonky**.

businessman battles behemoth bluster

balderdash (BOLL-der-dash) *noun*
nonsense or exaggeration. If your friend says, "I can run
a mile in under three and a half minutes," you should
respond, "Balderdash!" (since you know full well that
Hicham El Guerrouj of Morocco ran the fastest mile ever—
just over three minutes and 43 seconds—in Rome on July 7,
1999). See also **codswallop, hogwash,** and **malarkey.**

ballyhoo (BA-lee-HOO) *noun*
a commotion created to attract attention; over-the-top
advertising, like the kind heard at circuses and carnivals

bamboozle (bam-BOOZ-uhl) *verb*
to deceive or throw off; to make a fool of
someone; to "pull the wool over their eyes"

bandwagon (BAND-wag-un) *noun*
a popular trend or idea. If people are "jumping on the
bandwagon," it means they are following the same trend at
the same time—depending on the bandwagon, that could be
a good thing or a bad thing.

barnstormer (BARN-storm-er) *noun*
a person who travels around the country putting on performances, such as a pilot who gives stunt-flying shows or a baseball player who plays in exhibition games

barrage (buh-RAJ) *noun*
a lot of something happening all at once. It usually refers to a blast of rapid gunfire, but it can also refer to a verbal outburst, like a barrage of insults.

bedevil (bee-DEV-uhl) *verb*
to possess, perplex, or bewitch someone; to cause confusion or to hamper

behemoth **(buh-HEE-muth)** *noun, adjective*
something (usually an animal) that is larger than life
and bigger than big, as in "The museum's replica of the
Tyrannosaurus rex was behemoth."

behoove (bee-HOOV) *verb*
to be necessary or proper, referring to something that is
in your best interest, if you know what's good for you; usually used in sentences that begin with "it," as in "It would
behoove you to remove your flamingo from my swimming
pool before I call the zoo."

bellicose (BEH-lih-kose) *adjective*
quarrelsome; this is a good way to describe someone who
likes to start an argument

besmirch (bee-SMERCH) *verb*
to make something dirty—but not in the way your clothes
get dirty when you play soccer in the mud. It means to
"dirty" or ruin someone's good name or reputation, usually
by saying bad stuff about them behind their back. "I'll never
forgive you for besmirching my reputation in this manner!"

betwixt (bee-TWIKST) *adverb, preposition*
another way of saying between. The phrase "betwixt and
between" means stuck in the middle, neither here nor there.

B

is for

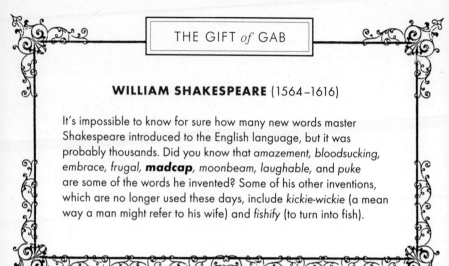

THE GIFT *of* GAB

WILLIAM SHAKESPEARE (1564–1616)

It's impossible to know for sure how many new words master Shakespeare introduced to the English language, but it was probably thousands. Did you know that *amazement, bloodsucking, embrace, frugal, **madcap**, moonbeam, laughable,* and *puke* are some of the words he invented? Some of his other inventions, which are no longer used these days, include *kickie-wickie* (a mean way a man might refer to his wife) and *fishify* (to turn into fish).

bevy (BEH-vee) *noun*
a large group, usually of people or quail or really anything at all. You could have a bevy of marbles, a bevy of socks, or even a bevy of **buccaneers**.

blarney (BLAR-nee) *noun*
flattery or nonsense. Legend has it that if you kiss the Blarney stone (in Ireland), you'll walk away with the gift of gab and be a smooth talker. To "tip the blarney" means to tell a fabulous (and probably not quite true) story.

boondoggle (BOON-dog-uhl) *noun, verb*
As a noun, *boondoggle* is a wasteful activity or work done for no reason other than to look busy (also known as "busywork"); as a verb, it means to deceive.

braggadocio (bra-guh-DOH-see-oh) *noun*
a braggart or show-off. Braggadocios assume you love them as much as they love themselves. The character Braggadocchio is a vain and boastful knight in the epic poem *The Faerie Queene* by Edmund Spenser.

brouhaha (BROO-ha-ha) *noun*
a whole lot of uproar, confusion, or excitement. If you want to save yourself a syllable, just say "hubbub" instead.

buccaneer (buk-uh-NEER) *noun*
a pirate. In the late seventeenth century, *buccaneer* referred specifically to a pirate who attacked Spanish ships. See also **landlubber** and **swashbuckler**.

capricious clowns

cacophony (kuh-KOFF-uh-nee) *noun*
a horrible mixture of sounds, such as the mixture of a
vacuum cleaner, a phone ringing, and a baby crying. It's the
kind of din that makes grown-ups ask, "Can you keep it down
to a dull roar?"

cahoots (kuh-HOOTS) *noun*
a very particular type of partnership. When you say that
two people are "in cahoots," it usually means that they are
up to no good.

cantankerous (kan-TANK-er-us) *adjective*
difficult to deal with. If there is a cantankerous old coot
living in the mansion up on the hill, it would **behoove** you not
to ring his doorbell and run away. See also **curmudgeon**.

capricious (kuh-PREE-shus) *adjective*
impulsive, like when you change your mind on a whim, or
unpredictable, like when you're teetering on the edge of
disaster

carbuncular (kar-BUNK-yoo-ler) *adjective*
A carbuncle is a gross, pus-filled skin infection, which makes
for a great insult: "I wouldn't expect anything to register in
that carbuncular brain of yours!"

catawampus (ka-tuh-WOMP-us) *adjective*
crooked, **askew**, or diagonally opposite,
just like **kitty-corner**

caterwaul (KA-ter-woll) *verb*
to wail noisily, or to complain loudly,
or to do both at the same time. At one
time, this meant to prowl the night
looking for mischief, much like a cat.

cavalcade (KA-vuhl-kade) *noun*
Originally, this was a procession of riders on horseback,
but these days a cavalcade is any kind of parade.

cavalier (ka-vuh-LEER) *adjective, noun*
As an adjective, this describes a dismissive attitude toward
serious or important matters (see also **laissez-faire**); as a
noun, this is an honorable and gallant man, such as a knight.

charlatan (SHAR-luh-tun) *noun*
a fake, phony, or imposter; someone who pretends to have
skills in order to impress or swindle people

c
is for

chartreuse (shar-TROOS) *noun*
a quite startling shade of yellow green

A HORSE OF A DIFFERENT COLOR . . .

aubergine (oh-ber-JZEEN): *very dark purple*
heliotrope (HEEL-ee-oh-trope): *reddish purple*
periwinkle (PARE-ee-ween-kuhl): *purplish blue*
vermilion (ver-MILL-yun): *bright red*

chutzpah (HUTS-pah) *noun*
a whole lot of confidence in yourself and your abilities;
audacity. The Cowardly Lion went looking for it, the Road
Runner had way too much of it for Wile E. Coyote's taste,
and Icarus (the mythological guy whose homemade wings
melted when he flew too close to the Sun) came to a pretty
sticky end because of it. See also **gumption** and **moxie**.

claptrap (KLAP-trap) *noun*
an old theater term that means a showy or insincere way to
encourage applause; these days it means a load of nonsense.
See also **codswallop** and **flapdoodle**.

cockamamie (KAH-kuh-MAY-mee) *adjective*
It sounds naughty, but it's not. It means ridiculous or pointless, as in, "Of all the cockamamie ideas you've spouted, this
is by far the worst."

c

is for

codswallop (KODS-woll-up) *noun*
yet another load of nonsense

comeuppance (kum-UP-ens) *noun*
a punishment that's completely deserved. If you behave
badly at dinnertime, you might get your comeuppance by
being denied dessert.

CONNIPTION (kuh-NIP-shun) *noun*

a tantrum or an angry outburst. Much worse than a hissy
fit, a conniption is especially dangerous (for you) when had
by your mom or teacher or someone of that **ilk**. This would
not be the time to tell such a person, "Don't get your underwear in a twist."

by Lewis Carroll, 1871
—*From Through the Looking-Glass, and What Alice Found There,*

"Contrariwise," continued Tweedledee, "if it was so, it might be;
and if it were so, it would be: but as it isn't, it ain't. That's logic."

contrariwise (KON-trayr-ee-wize) *adverb*
behaving in a fickle and contrary manner;
deliberately taking the opposite point of view

conundrum (kuh-NUN-drum) *noun*
any kind of brain-stretching riddle or question. Here's one
that'll keep you guessing (or not!): What occurs once in a
minute and twice in a moment, but never in a hundred years?
It's quite a conundrum, isn't it?

crapshoot (KRAP-shoot) *noun*
This sounds dirty too, but it's not. This is another way to say
gamble, something with an unpredictable outcome.

crux (CRUKS) *noun*
the central point; the most important element, as in "the crux
of the situation"

curmudgeon (ker-MUDJ-un) *noun*
a grumpy and opinionated person. The curmudgeon's
archenemy is the young **whippersnapper**.

dillydallying ducky

dalliance (DA-lee-yuns) *noun*
a trifling, frivolous activity, often with amorous intent
(and therefore usually conducted with another person)

dastardly (DAS-terd-lee) *adjective*
sneaky or underhanded. Dick Dastardly is the name of a
cartoon villain created in the 1960s. He has a long, thin
mustache, which all dastardly villains need for twirling as
they hatch their **diabolical** schemes.

debacle (deh-BAH-kuhl) *noun*
a disaster or failure. For example: "Our parents still give
us a hard time about that human-cannonball-off-the-roof
debacle."

WORD PLAY

A palindrome is a word or series of words that can be read the same
forward and backward. One of the most well-known palindromes is
"A man, a plan, a canal—Panama!"

D

is for

Dastardly Debonair Disheveled

debonair (deh-buh-NARE) *adjective*
stylish, suave, dapper, well-put-together; usually used
to describe a handsomely dressed man

derring-do (DARE-eeng-DOO) *noun*
heroic or daring deeds. So basically, if someone tells you,
"Wow, I'm impressed by your heroic feats of derring-do,"
they are telling you that your courageous actions of daring
deeds were very heroic.

diabolical (dy-uh-BOLL-ih-kuhl) *adjective*
describes the type of devilish, fiendish, or wicked things
that a **dastardly** person would do. If some dastardly person
ruins your life, the most natural thing for you to do is shake
your fist and shout, "Diabolical!"

D

is for

THE GIFT *of* GAB

CHARLES DICKENS (1812–1870)

Charles Dickens is famous for creating characters with weird and wonderful names, some of which have become adjectives that are still used today. *Pickwickian*, from the character Samuel Pickwick of *Pickwick Papers*, describes someone who is very honest and generous. *Pecksniffian*, from the character Seth Pecksniff of *Martin Chuzzlewit*, describes a person who smugly criticizes someone for doing something—and then does the very same thing himself.

didgeridoo (did-jer-ee-DOO) *noun*
a long, trumpetlike instrument made of wood or bamboo.
Created by the Aborigines (the native people of Australia),
the didgeridoo was probably named after the sound it makes
(with a lot of emphasis on the "-doo" part of the word).

AND SPEAKING OF INSTRUMENTS . . .

flugelhorn (FLOO-guhl-horn): *a brass instrument*

glockenspiel (GLOK-en-shpeel): *a percussion instrument played with two hammers*

hurdy-gurdy (HER-dee-GER-dee): *a stringed instrument played by turning a crank*

ukulele (yoo-kuh-LAY-lee): *a small guitar with four strings*

xylophone (ZY-luh-fone): *a percussion instrument played with wooden hammers*

zither (ZIH-ther): *a stringed instrument with 30 to 40 strings played with pick and fingers*

dilapidated (dih-LAP-uh-day-tid) *adjective*
run-down, falling apart, the worse for wear, perhaps
even looking like something the cat dragged in, although
it is usually used to describe buildings or cars, things that
a normal-sized cat would never be able to drag around

dillydally (DILL-ee-dall-ee) *verb*
to waste time, dawdle, dither. See also **lollygag**.

discombobulated (diss-kum-BOB-yoo-lay-tid) *adjective*
upset, confused, or out of sorts, as in "I don't know what's
wrong with me. I've felt discombobulated all day."

disheveled (dih-SHEV-uhld) *adjective*
in disorder or disarray. It comes from the Middle English
word *discheveled*, meaning disordered hair. These days,
however, when people refer to a "disheveled appearance,"
they mean more than just an untidy hairstyle.

doldrums (DOLE-drumz) *noun*
a period of sadness or listlessness; the feeling of being
down in the dumps

In Norton Juster's novel The Phantom Tollbooth, *Milo (the hero)
finds himself stuck in a lethargic land called the Doldrums. The
only way he can escape is through the power of positive thinking.*

doppelgänger (DOP-uhl-gang-er) *noun*
the ghostly counterpart of a living person, like a super-
natural evil twin. Some people believe that every person
in the world has a doppelgänger, but it might just be soap-
opera characters.

druthers (DRUH-therz) *noun*
a choice that's completely unrestricted, as in "If I had my
druthers, I would run away and join the circus." The spelling
comes from combining the words *would* and *rather*.

duck soup (DUK SOOP) *noun*
something easy to do; similar to
the expression "piece of cake"

Duck Soup *is a famous movie
from 1933, starring the Marx
brothers. They also made a
movie called* **Horse Feathers**.
Go figure!

dungarees (dun-guh-REEZ) *noun*
an old-timey word for jeans; dungaree is a heavy cotton
fabric woven from colored yarns. Nowadays, dungarees are
a pair of pants held up by straps that pass over the shoulders
and fasten to a bib in the front (aka overalls). See page 67 for
some more fun, wearable words.

enigmatic elephant

egads! (ee-GADZ) *interjection*
not a swearword, but something better than "Gosh!" or
"Darn it!" to say when you're excited, shocked, or creeped
out. See also **gadzooks!** and the list on the next page for
other things you can shout when you stub your toe or get
locked out of your house wearing only your underwear.

*"It is a riddle,
wrapped in a mystery,
inside an enigma."
— Winston Churchill, 1939*

enigma (eh-NIG-muh) *noun*
something that's almost impossible
to understand or explain; usually
refers to a mysterious person

ensconce (en-SKONS) *verb*
to be sheltered or to settle down
comfortably. You can be
ensconced in a big,
puffy coat or in a
tree house, but you
probably wouldn't
consider yourself
ensconced if you
were on a bed of
nails or in the
dentist's chair.

OODLES OF INTERJECTIONS AND EXCLAMATIONS }

Blimey!

Bust my buttons!

By Jove!

Crikey!

Criminy!

Curses!

Dagnabit!

For crying out loud!

For goodness' sake!

For Pete's sake!

Gee whillikers!

Gee whiz!

Geez Louise!

Goodness gracious!

Good night nurse!

Goody gumdrops!

Great Scott!

Heavens to Betsy!

Holy cow!

Holy mackerel!

Holy moly!

Holy Toledo!

Hot diggety dog!

Huzzah!

Jeepers!

Jiminy Cricket!

Jinkies!

Jumpin' Jehoshaphat!

Land's sakes!

Leapin' lizards!

Pshaw!

Sake's alive!

What in Sam Hill?!

What in tarnation?!

What the devil?!

Whoa Nellie!

Yikes!

Yowza!

Zoinks!

E
is for

elegant equestrian

erstwhile (ERST-wile) *adjective, adverb*
former or in the past, such as an erstwhile friend or an erstwhile hairdo

eschew (eh-SHOO) *verb*
to purposely avoid or keep away from something. You might be the type of person to eschew Brussels sprouts or laundry, or perhaps you choose to eschew people who use the word *eschew.*

extemporaneous (ex-tem-por-AY-nee-us) *adjective*
spur of the moment, on the fly, makeshift. If you get caught in a lie or someone challenges you to back up your statement, you could fend them off by replying, "Oh, never mind, that was just an extemporaneous observation."

extrapolate (ex-TRA-poh-late) *verb*
to make a guess based on the information you have. Mathematicians do a lot of extrapolating.

extravaganza (ex-tra-vuh-GAN-zuh) *noun*
a lavish, loud, and colorful event. This is a word that sounds best when drawn out: "This is going to be the biggest extravagaaanzaa of the year!"

fantastic flyer

fandango (fan-DANE-goh) *noun*
a fast Spanish dance performed by a man and a
woman, accompanied by a guitar and castanets. If you hear
the word and there's nobody dancing, somebody's probably
talking about **tomfoolery**.

fare-thee-well (FARE-thee-well) *noun*
total perfection or the highest degree. On the other hand, the
phrase "fare thee well" (without the hyphens) is a way of
saying good-bye and "may you fare well."

fiddlesticks! (FIH-duhl-stiks) *interjection*
that's nonsense! (But if it's just one fiddlestick, then it's the
bow that plays a violin.)

F

is for

~~~~~⟨∞⟩~~~~~

finagle (fih-NAY-guhl) *verb*
When you get something by devious means, you're guilty of finagling. (It just sounds less sneaky than "tricking.")

fisticuffs (FIS-tih-kufs) *noun*
a fistfight. A polite way to respond to a bully would be "I don't care to engage in fisticuffs with a **hooligan** such as you." See also **pugilist**.

THEM'S FIGHTIN' WORDS!

altercation	(oll-ter-KAY-shun)
brawl	(BROLL)
donnybrook	(DON-ee-bruhk)
fracas	(FRA-kus)
free-for-all	(FREE-fer-oll)
knock-down-drag-out	(NOK-down-DRAG-owt)
scrap	(SKRAP)
scrimmage	(SKRIM-ij)
scuffle	(SKUFF-uhl)
skirmish	(SKER-mish)
squabble	(SKWAH-buhl)
wrangle	(RANE-guhl)

flabbergast (FLAB-er-gast) *verb*
to overwhelm with shock or surprise. You can be flabbergasted in a good way ("Maddy was flabbergasted when she received her test score") or a bad way ("Maddy was flabbergasted when she received her test score").

F
is for

flapdoodle (FLAP-doo-duhl) *noun*
nonsense; foolish talk

flibbertigibbet (FLIH-ber-tee-jih-bit) *noun*
a silly word for a silly person; a gossip or an overly talkative
person; someone who is flighty, unreliable, and scatterbrained

flimflam (FLIM-flam) *noun*
nonsense created with the intention to deceive or swindle
somebody

flotsam (FLOT-sum) *noun*
wreckage from a ship that's found floating on the water's
surface; also used to mean anything that's of no use. See also
jetsam.

flummox (FLUM-uks) *verb*
to confuse. Instead of saying, "I'm confused" or "Beats me,"
spice things up with "It's sure got me flummoxed!"

fuddy-duddy (FUH-dee-DUH-dee) *noun*
a crabby, old-fashioned, or uptight person; a stick-in-the-mud

fussbudget (FUSS-buj-it) *noun*
someone who fusses too much. Fussbudgets and **fuddy-duddies**
can often be found in the company of **curmudgeons**. See also
persnickety.

G
is for

gallant girl

gadabout (GA-duh-bowt) *noun*
someone who flits around from place to place, like a
social butterfly but more restless. Gadabouts have a
tendency to **gallivant**.

gadzooks! (gad-ZOOKS) *interjection*
an old-timey expression of surprise, similar to "What the
devil?!" See also **egads!** and **fiddlesticks!** and the list on
page 32.

gallivant (GAL-ih-vant) *verb*
to travel around for pleasure; usually used in a negative way
to accuse someone of being irresponsible, as in "While you
were out gallivanting, I was stuck here building this tandem
bicycle by myself!"

galoot (guh-LOOT) *noun*
a foolish, awkward, and clumsy person ("Ya big galoot!");
also a nickname for someone who is an **aficionado** or
collector of woodworking tools

galumph (guh-LUMF) *verb*
to move in a heavy-footed
way. Things that may galumph:
elephants, Frankenstein's
monster, the Abominable
Snowman, and people com-
peting in a three-legged race.
Not surprisingly, a "gollumpus"
is a large, clumsy fellow.

Lewis Carroll invented the word
galumph *by combining* gallop *and*
triumph. *He also invented the word*
chortle *by combining* chuckle *and* snort.

galvanize (GAL-vuh-nize) *verb*
to motivate into action. The original, scientific meaning of
galvanize is to stimulate with an electric current. It also
means to cover something made of iron or steel with a coat-
ing of zinc.

"As for you, my galvanized friend, you want a heart?
You don't know how lucky you are not to have one."
—*From the movie* The Wizard of Oz, *1939*

gangbusters (GAYNG-bus-terz) *noun*
Originally, gangbusters were the people who were in charge
of busting up criminal gangs, but now the word describes
anything that is done with speed and enthusiasm. *Gang
Busters* was a popular radio show that began in the 1930s.
Each episode began with loud sound effects, such as bullets
firing and tires screeching, so people soon began describing
anything loud and forceful as being "like Gang Busters."

gangway (GAYNG-way) *noun, interjection*
another word for *gangplank*, which is a temporary
passageway created by laying down planks. *Gangway* is also
a useful thing to shout out when you're trying to clear your
way through a crowd.

garrulous (GARE-uh-liss) *adjective*
talkative in a roundabout way; rambling and wordy

gauntlet (GAWNT-let) *noun*
a metal glove, part of the armor worn by knights. Back in
the day, if a knight was offended, he would throw down
his gauntlet and challenge the offender to a fight. To "run
the gauntlet" means to endure a series of ordeals or
punishments.

ghastly (GAST-lee) *adjective*
horrific, frightening, or simply unpleasant. Things that can
be ghastly: the scene of a murder, the color of vomit, and
your sister's new haircut.

gibberish (JIH-ber-ish) *noun*
language that sounds like English but doesn't actually mean
anything; frequently heard when discussing technical or
scientific things. According to one theory, the word comes
from an eighth-century alchemist named Geber who invented
a code language in order to keep his work secret.

gizzard (GIH-zerd) *noun*
a part of the digestive system (innards, guts) of many
creatures—including birds, reptiles, earthworms, and
some insects—that's used to grind up food

WORD PLAY

There are at least six accepted pronunciations of the letter combination *ough*, and you can hear all six if you read this sentence aloud: When the bough broke, the cradle did fall, and then down came baby, through the store-bought door, and into the rough ball of dough, where she was found coughing and sneezing.

glad-hand (GLAD-hand) *verb*
to schmooze with people and act glad to shake their hands, usually when trying to win votes or get on someone's good side

gobbledygook (GAH-buhl-dee-guhk) *noun*
wordy and hard-to-understand jargon, as in "Much to Sam's dismay, the instructions that came with his new helicopto-robot were gobbledygook." See also **gibberish**.

gonzo (GON-zoh) *adjective*
bizarre or unconventional, or using an exaggerated style; also a type of journalism in which the reporter puts him- or herself in the story and mixes fact with fiction

> *"I shall now recite from the works of Percy Bysshe Shelley while, and at the same time, defusing this highly explosive bomb."*
> —*Gonzo (the Muppet)*

goulash (GOO-losh) *noun*
a Hungarian stew made with meat and vegetables; *goulash* is often used to mean any kind of jumble. See also **hodgepodge**.

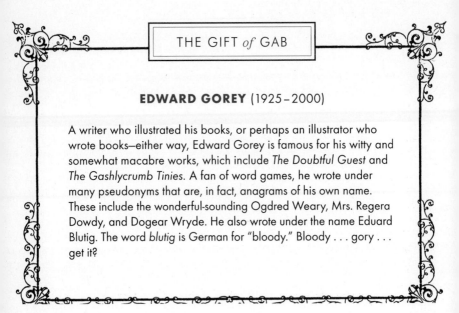

THE GIFT *of* GAB

EDWARD GOREY (1925–2000)

A writer who illustrated his books, or perhaps an illustrator who wrote books—either way, Edward Gorey is famous for his witty and somewhat macabre works, which include *The Doubtful Guest* and *The Gashlycrumb Tinies*. A fan of word games, he wrote under many pseudonyms that are, in fact, anagrams of his own name. These include the wonderful-sounding Ogdred Weary, Mrs. Regera Dowdy, and Dogear Wryde. He also wrote under the name Eduard Blutig. The word *blutig* is German for "bloody." Bloody . . . gory . . . get it?

gravy train (GRAY-vee trane) *noun*
a situation that will lead to easy money. As a slang word, *gravy* means something easy to do or something with unexpected value. If you're "ridin' the gravy train," you should hold on tight, because you could fall off at any moment.

gumption (GUMP-shun) *noun*
This is what you get when you mix courage and initiative and add a smidge of recklessness. See also **chutzpah** and **moxie**.

gumshoe (GUM-shoo) *noun*
slang word for a detective. The word comes from the
soft-soled shoes made of gum rubber that were popular
in the late 1800s. As they were rather more quiet than their
leather-soled counterparts, the verb *gumshoe* came to mean
"to sneak around." Oddly, *gumshoe* originally meant a thief
(because thieves sneak around in order to prey on their vic-
tims); only later was it used for someone (like a detective)
who sneaks around in order to catch thieves.

harried hare

haberdasher
(HA-ber-dash-er) *noun*
someone who sells men's
clothing and accessories. After
stopping by the haberdasher's, you might
pop into the apothecary (pharmacy) and then visit
the cobbler (shoe repair). In the eighteenth century, a
slang description for a schoolteacher was "haberdasher of
nouns and pronouns."

hackneyed (HAK-need) *adjective*
stale, boring, done to death

hanker (HANK-er) *verb*
to yearn or have a real longing or desire for something. You
might be hankering for a glass of cold lemonade or some
peanut-butter cups.

happenstance (HAP-in-stans) *noun*
A combination of the words *happen* and *circumstance*, this
means something that occurs entirely due to chance.

> "Once is happenstance. Twice is coincidence.
> The third time it's enemy action."
> —From Goldfinger, *by Ian Fleming, 1959*

harangue (huh-RAYNG) *noun*
a long (and often scolding) speech or lecture

harbinger (HAR-bin-jer) *noun*
a pioneer of change. If you hear the phrase "harbinger
of doom," it refers to something whose presence foretells
unpleasantness to come. Ooh, chilling.

harum-scarum (HARE-um-SKARE-um) *adjective*
Harum Scarum is an Elvis Presley movie, but *harum-scarum*
means reckless and careless.

haymaker (HAY-may-ker) *noun*
a slang term for a curving and powerful punch, maybe
because the curve of this punch resembles the swing of a
scythe (a tool used to cut hay), or perhaps because such
a powerful punch to the face would leave it looking cut up
like hay

heave-ho (HEEV-hoh) *noun*
a dismissal. You might give an unappealing boyfriend (or
girlfriend) "the old heave-ho," which is to say you would
end the relationship. It was originally a nautical
expression—a command to sailors to pull on a rope.

heebie-jeebies (HEE-bee-JEE-bees) *noun*
Invented by Billy DeBeck, a famous cartoonist of the 1920s,
this is a feeling of apprehension, somewhat like "the jitters."
It's always used in the plural form, although, perhaps, a
single heebie-jeebie might be less worrisome.

helter-skelter (HEL-ter-SKEL-ter) *adverb*
in disorder or confusion; haphazard. In Great Britain,
a helter-skelter is a long fairground slide with twists
and turns.

hem and haw (HEM and HAH) *verb*
You're hemming and hawing whenever you cough and clear
your throat in order to buy time after being asked a question.

histrionics (hiss-tree-ON-iks) *noun*
dramatic and exaggerated behavior, as in "There's really no
need for these histrionics!" See also **conniption**.

hobgoblin (HOB-gob-lin) *noun*
an especially naughty and **bedeviling** type of goblin.
Hobgoblins have appeared in folktales since the sixteenth
century.

H

is for

hocus-pocus (HOH-kiss-POH-kiss) *noun*
clever tricks or nonsense presented as truth. **Charlatans**
often use a lot of hocus-pocus to **bamboozle** their audiences.

hodgepodge (HOJ-poj) *noun*
a mixed-up jumble of all kinds of things. It comes from the
word *hotchpotch*, which is a thick soup or stew.

hogwash (HOG-wosh) *noun*
and yet another word for nonsense. See also **balderdash,
codswallop, humbug, jabberwocky**, and **malarkey**.

hoi polloi (HOY puh-LOY) *noun*
the people, the multitude, the madding crowd, as in
"Let's eat lunch in the library so we can get away from
the hoi polloi."

WORDPLAY

The longest place name in the United States is
Lake Chargoggagoggmanchauggagoggchaubunagungamaugg,
in Webster, Massachusetts. (You're on your own for pronunciation.)

hoity-toity (HOY-tee-TOY-tee) *adjective, noun*
When this word first appeared in the late seventeenth
century, it was a noun meaning silly, flighty behavior.
By the eighteenth century, it was being used to describe
people who are rather self-important and who think of
themselves as "a cut above" everybody else.

HOOLIGANISM (HOO-lih-guh-nizm) *noun*
rowdy or unruly behavior, such as **fisticuffs**, vandalism,
and other destructive activities. Hooligans are people
who engage in hooliganism.

hootenanny (HOO-tih-nah-nee) *noun*
a folk-music concert, often with audience members
participating

hornswoggle
(HORN-swah-guhl) *verb*
to deceive, cheat, or
bamboozle

"We're hornswoggled.
We're backed to a standstill.
We're double-crossed
to a fare-you-well."
—From Valley of the Moon,
by Jack London, 1913

horsefeathers! (HORS-feh-therz) *interjection*
rubbish, nonsense, not even worth thinking about

hullabaloo (HUH-luh-buh-loo) *noun*
a loud and annoying noise, oftentimes caused by a group
of unruly children. See also **ruckus**.

humbug (HUM-bug) *noun*
nonsense. In Charles Dickens's *A Christmas Carol*, everyone's
favorite **curmudgeon**, Ebenezer Scrooge, is fond of saying
"Bah, humbug" to convey his disbelief or dislike of the cheerful
celebrations of Christmas.

*"How can I help being a humbug," he said, "when all these people
make me do things that everybody knows can't be done?"*
—From *The Wonderful Wizard of Oz*, by L. Frank Baum, 1902

humdinger (HUM-DING-er) *noun*
something that's quite extraordinary, usually preceded
by an interjection like "wow" or "gosh," as in "Wow, that
pumpkin of yours is quite a humdinger!" It sounds best
when you draw out the first syllable: "huuum-dinger!"

hunky-dory (hun-kee-DOR-ee) *adjective*
something that's just right in a rather perfect kind of way.
That last bowl of porridge was just hunky-dory for Goldilocks.

hurly-burly (HER-lee-BER-lee) *noun*
a noisy uproar

imperiled insect

I
is for

ilk (ILK) *noun*
sort, kind, or nature, as in "I refuse to eat pumpkin, zucchini, or anything of that ilk."

imbroglio (im-BROLE-yoh) *noun*
a scandal or a complicated situation or misunderstanding. See also **brouhaha**.

impresario (im-prih-SAR-ee-oh) *noun*
a person who puts on shows. An impresario would probably use a lot of **ballyhoo** to attract guests.

incognito (in-cog-NEE-toh) *adjective, adverb, noun*
(*incog* for short) undercover, in disguise. You can "go incog" to slip past your adoring fans (or loathing enemies) unnoticed.

indubitably (in-DOO-bih-tuh-blee) *adverb*
definitely, without a doubt, no question about it. And how!

> "You know, you can say it backwards,
> which is 'dociousaliexpiisticfragilcalirupus,'
> but that's going a bit too far, don't you think?"
> "Indubitably!"
> —From the movie *Mary Poppins*, 1964

inkling (EENK-leeng) *noun*
a very slight hint or clue, as in "I haven't an inkling why you're so angry. It's not even my flamingo!"

interloper (IN-ter-loh-per) *noun*
someone who intrudes, invades, or horns in where he or
she is not expected or welcome

irk (ERK) *verb*
to irritate or annoy. A polite
way to express that you're
ticked off would be "Oh man,
I am really irked. I am peeved
to a **fare-thee-well**."

irked infant

jabberwocky (JAB-er-wok-ee) *noun*
yet another word for nonsense. "Jabberwocky" is the title of
a nonsense poem written by Lewis Carroll in 1871.

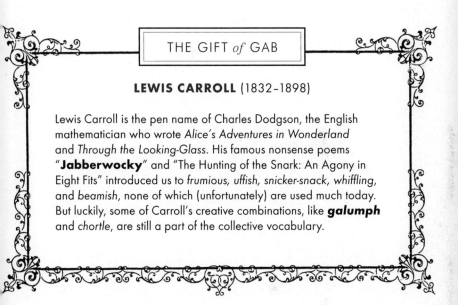

THE GIFT *of* GAB

LEWIS CARROLL (1832–1898)

Lewis Carroll is the pen name of Charles Dodgson, the English
mathematician who wrote *Alice's Adventures in Wonderland*
and *Through the Looking-Glass*. His famous nonsense poems
"**Jabberwocky**" and "The Hunting of the Snark: An Agony in
Eight Fits" introduced us to *frumious, uffish, snicker-snack, whiffling,*
and *beamish,* none of which (unfortunately) are used much today.
But luckily, some of Carroll's creative combinations, like ***galumph***
and *chortle,* are still a part of the collective vocabulary.

jack-of-all-trades (JAK-uv-oll-TRAYDZ) *noun*
someone who can do all kinds of work. The word *jack* is
a bit of a jack-of-all-trades itself: Jack Frost, lumberjack,
crackerjack, jackknife, jackpot, jumping jack, jackhammer,
jack-in-the-pulpit . . .

jalopy (juh-LOP-ee) *noun*
a beat-up old car

jambalaya (jam-buh-LY-uh) *noun*
a Cajun dish of rice, ham, sausage, chicken, and shrimp.
It's also come to mean something similar to **goulash** or a
mixture of different things.

SOUNDS FUN ENOUGH TO EAT . . .

cacciatore (cach-uh-TOR-ee): *cooked with tomatoes and herbs*
Gorgonzola (gor-gun-ZOH-luh): *a type of cheese*
hasenpfeffer (HOSS-en-feff-er): *a rabbit stew*
mulligatawny (mull-ih-guh-TAWN-ee): *a curry-flavored chicken soup*
snicker doodle (SNIK-er DOO-duhl): *a type of cookie*

J

is for

jamboree (jam-bor-EE) *noun*
a gathering that is filled with fun and good humor.
The Boy Scouts call their national meetings jamborees.

jetsam (JET-sum) *noun*
anything that's thrown from a ship in order to lighten its
load. *Jetsam* is an alteration of *jettison*, a verb that means to
get rid of something that's a burden. See also **flotsam**.

jittery-skittery (JIT-er-ee-SKIT-er-ee) *adjective*
feeling panicky or nervous. See also **heebie-jeebies**.

Johnny-on-the-spot (JON-ee-on-thuh-SPOT) *noun*
someone who is always there when you need him (or her);
someone who is in the right place at the right time. On the
flip side, a Johnny-come-lately is someone who hasn't been
around long or is "late to the party," that is, out of the loop
and not up to speed.

jubilation (JOO-buh-LAY-shun) *noun*
lots of happiness and rejoicing

juggernaut (JUG-er-not) *noun*
a huge unstoppable force that will crush anything in its path,
such as *Star Wars* fans

juxtaposition (juks-tuh-puh-ZISH-un) *noun*
the side-by-side appearance of things. You might agree that
the juxtaposition of a **chartreuse** scarf with a pink sweater
would be pretty **ghastly**.

kamikaze (kom-ih-KOZ-ee) *noun, adjective*
During World War II, kamikazes were Japanese fighter pilots. These days the word *kamikaze* is used to describe a dangerous and reckless action or someone who engages in such dangerous actions without thinking of the consequences.

kaput (kuh-PUHT) *adjective*
done, over, finished, finito, no more, lifeless, ceased to be, and so on and so forth

katzenjammer (KATS-in-jam-er) *noun*
uneasiness or distress; a loud noise or uproar. *The Katzenjammer Kids* is a very long-running comic strip about two rebellious boys named Hans and Fritz.

kerfuffle (ker-FUF-uhl) *noun*
a big fuss. See also **brouhaha**.

kibosh (KY-bosh or kih-BOSH) *noun*
something that puts a stop to something else. The phrase
"put the kibosh on" has been around since the early 1800s,
and it means to stop something dead in its tracks (similar
to "nip it in the bud").

kilter (KIL-ter) *noun*
the usual or good condition, so to be off-kilter is to be
unusual or in bad condition

kit and caboodle (KIT and kuh-BOO-duhl) *noun*
Both *kit* and *caboodle* are words that mean a collection or
group of something, so putting them together just emphasizes
the point: the whole darn lot of it.

kitty-corner (KIT-ee-kor-ner) *adverb, adjective*
located opposite or diagonally; it is an alteration of the word
catercorner

WORD PLAY

A pangram is a sentence that uses every letter of the alphabet. The most
famous pangram is "The quick brown fox jumps over the lazy dog," which
was popularized in the nineteenth century by the telegraph company
Western Union when they used it to test the accuracy of the company's
equipment.

knickerbockers (NIK-er-bok-erz) *noun*
knee-length pants; a slang word for people from New York.
The word comes from Diedrich Knickerbocker, the fictional
author of *History of New York*, published in 1809, which
was really written by Washington Irving. The connection
between the word and the book? Knickerbocker's book has
illustrations of Dutchmen wearing short pants!

knickknack (NIK-nak) *noun*
a bauble, trinket, or other little ornamental item that's
not worth very much money (although it may have
sentimental value for the owner). Not only does
this word begin and end with the letter K, it has
a double dose of it in the middle! See also **tchotchke**.

kowtow (KOW-tow) *verb*
to act in a very humble and overly respectful way; in other,
more colloquial words, to suck up to somebody

laissez-faire (leh-zay-FARE) *adjective*
having a "whatever happens, happens" attitude. The translation of this French verb is "to let people do as they wish." The word came about to describe a style of government that supports freedom of choice, but these days people can be called laissez-faire if they don't get involved with other people's business.

landlubber (LAND-luh-ber) *noun*
someone who is more comfortable on dry land. Experienced sailors might tease you if your landlubberness is showing.

THE GIFT *of* GAB

EDWARD LEAR (1812–1888)

This English writer and illustrator is famous for his nonsense verse. His most popular poem is "The Owl and the Pussycat" and it ends like this:

> *They dined on mince, and slices of quince,*
> *Which they ate with a runcible spoon.*

Runcible, a word invented by Lear, is now part of the English language. It is a utensil that is a combination of knife, fork, and spoon.

layabout (LAY-uh-bowt) *noun*
a lazy person; someone who just lies about not doing any work

lickety-split (lik-eh-tee-SPLIT) *adverb*
really fast. The word *split* is slang for "leave," as in "Let's split this place." Adding *lickety* makes the splitting faster. Other versions of this old-timey word include *lickety-click*, *lickety-cut*, and *lickety-switch*.

WORD PLAY

A lipogram is a sentence, paragraph, book, or other text in which the author has purposely refrained from using certain letters or words. Entire books have been written without using the letter E, which must have been difficult considering that E is the most common letter in the English language.

L
is for

lily-livered (LIL-ee-LIV-erd) *adjective*
cowardly. Back in the olden days, people thought the liver was
the source of human passions and emotions, such as courage.
A red-blooded liver was a healthy one, but a white-as-a-lily
liver lacked strength and passion. See also **yellow-bellied**.

> *"Any one of you lily-livered, bowlegged varmints
> care to slap leather with me?"*
> —*Yosemite Sam*

linsey-woolsey (LIN-zee-WUHL-zee) *noun*
a thick and durable fabric made of wool and linen

{ ··········· **WEARABLE WORDS** } } ··············

crinoline (CRIN-oh-lin): *a stiff fabric for underskirts*
gabardine (ga-bar-DEEN): *a durable fabric*
galligaskins (gal-ih-GAS-kins): *very loose trousers*
houndstooth (HOWNDZ-tooth): *fabric with a broken-check pattern*
jodhpurs (JOD-pers): *special horseback-riding pants*
lederhosen (LEED-er-hoze-in): *leather shorts with suspenders*
organza (or-GAN-zuh): *sheer, stiff silk*
seersucker (SEER-suk-er): *a lightweight, puckered fabric*

logorrhea (lah-guh-REE-uh) *noun*
excessive talking that is usually incoherent and often
associated with mental illness; sometimes called verbal
diarrhea. See also **garrulous**.

lollapalooza (lol-uh-puh-LOO-zuh) *noun*
something (or somebody) that is outstanding
or extraordinary

L O L L Y G A G (LOL-ee-gag) *verb*
No, this doesn't have anything to do with choking on
a lollipop. It means to dawdle, waste time, lag behind,
and generally slow things down, basically the opposite
of **lickety-split**.

longshanks (LONG-shaynks) *noun*

nickname for a long-legged person. The shank is the part
of your leg between your knee and ankle. See also **spindle-
shanked**.

look-see (LUHK-see) *noun*

a quick inspection. Although it sounds redundant, it really
can be necessary to take a look *and* see what's going on.

loosey-goosey (LOO-see-GOO-see) *adjective*

calm and relaxed, often too much so. It comes from the
expression "loose as a goose," because as everyone knows
geese are really laid back. Things that can easily become
loosey-goosey include a person's attitude, appearance, and
commitment to turning homework in on time.

mobilized mutt

machinations (mash-uh-NAY-shuns or mak-uh-NAY-shuns) *noun*
complicated, and usually evil, plans. It's one of those words
that you tend to use in its plural form, perhaps because one
machination by itself wouldn't be scary enough.

madcap (MAD-kap) *adjective*
kooky, crazy, impulsive.
In the sixteenth century,
a madcap was an insane
person, like *madman*.
The *cap* bit of the word
refers to the head. Put it
together and you get
"someone who's mad in
the head."

maelstrom (MALE-strum) *noun*
a powerful whirlpool that sucks in objects; also used to mean anything that is turbulent, such as a "maelstrom of emotions"

malarkey (muh-LAR-kee) *noun*
nonsense or foolish talk. See also **flapdoodle**.

marauder (muh-RAH-der) *noun*
Besides being a type of muscle car and the nickname of a certain group of wizards, a marauder is a person who marauds, or roams about with the intent to attack and pillage.

mealy-mouthed (MEE-lee-mowtht) *adjective*
hypocritical or devious; describes someone who is too cowardly (or too sneaky) to be honest and say what he or she means

melee (MAY-lay) *noun*
a confused gaggle of people, as in "It took ages for us to fight our way through the melee after the concert let out."

milieu (mil-YOO) *noun*
your background or environment; the place where something thrives or develops

milquetoast (MILK-tohst) *noun*
a person who is timid or meek, who lets other people get away with things; a doormat. This word comes from the comic-strip character Caspar Milquetoast, created in 1924 by H. T. Webster.

mizzenmast (MIZ-en-mast) *noun*
a ship's third mast, which is one of the tall poles that support the yards, booms, and rigging (the ropes and sails)

mollycoddle (MAH-lee-kah-duhl) *verb, noun*
as a verb, this means to pamper or spoil someone, and
as a noun, this is that someone who is pampered or spoiled

monger (MON-ger) *noun*
somebody who sells something. You'll usually see this word
attached to another, such as *fishmonger* or *newsmonger*.

monkeyshines (MUN-kee-shynz) *noun*
pranks or mischievous acts; the expression "monkeying
around" means goofing off or wreaking havoc. See also
tomfoolery.

M

is for

*Invented in 1884, Moxie was a carbonated drink advertised
as a cure-all that would give you pep and energy.
Moxie is still around today, and it is the official state soft drink of Maine.*

moxie (MOK-see) *noun*
courage and determination; the nerve to do something,
as in "You got a lot of moxie, kid!" See also **gumption**.

muckety-muck (MUK-eh-tee-muk) *noun*
a **hoity-toity** bigwig, someone who thinks of themselves
as a big deal. And a high muckety-muck is an even bigger
deal. Other versions of this word include *muck-a-muck*
and *mucky-muck*.

mulligan (MUH-lih-gin) *noun*
a do-over. People might
"take a mulligan" in many
situations or games, but
it is especially common in
the game of golf. Of course,
mulligans are actually illegal
under the strict rules of the game.

mumbo-jumbo (MUM-boh JUM-boh) *noun*
unnecessarily complex language. This can also mean an
activity that's based on superstitious beliefs. Mumbo Jumbo
was the name of an African god, the worship of whom
mystified many nineteenth-century Europeans. See also
gobbledygook.

namby-pamby (NAM-bee-PAM-bee) *adjective*
weak and pointless; usually used to describe someone who
lacks substance. Namby Pamby was the mocking nickname
given to Ambrose Philips, a popular English poet in the
eighteenth century, by some other poets of his era, who may
have been jealous of his success (*Namby* being a less than
clever distortion of Ambrose).

ne'er-do-well (NARE-doo-well) *noun*
a good-for-nothing or worthless person; a goof-off, someone who "never does well." See also **layout**, **rapscallion**,
and **scalawag**.

newfangled (NOO-fane-guhld) *adjective*
a somewhat **curmudgeonly** way to describe the latest and
most up-to-date inventions. At one time, everyday objects
like televisions, washing machines, and automobiles were
considered newfangled and regarded with suspicion.

nickelodeon (nih-kuh-LOH-dee-yun) *noun*
a movie theater of the early twentieth century. It cost a
nickel to get in, which explains the name.

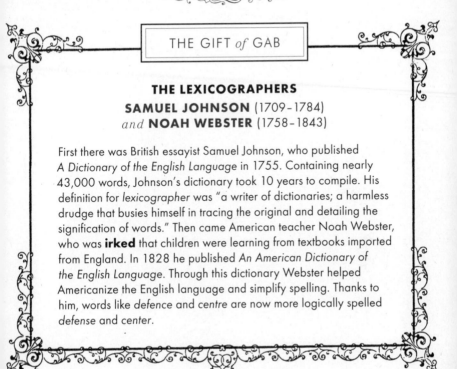

THE GIFT *of* GAB

THE LEXICOGRAPHERS
SAMUEL JOHNSON (1709–1784)
and NOAH WEBSTER (1758–1843)

First there was British essayist Samuel Johnson, who published *A Dictionary of the English Language* in 1755. Containing nearly 43,000 words, Johnson's dictionary took 10 years to compile. His definition for *lexicographer* was "a writer of dictionaries; a harmless drudge that busies himself in tracing the original and detailing the signification of words." Then came American teacher Noah Webster, who was **irked** that children were learning from textbooks imported from England. In 1828 he published *An American Dictionary of the English Language.* Through this dictionary Webster helped Americanize the English language and simplify spelling. Thanks to him, words like *defence* and *centre* are now more logically spelled *defense* and *center.*

nitty-gritty (NIH-tee-GRIH-tee) *noun, adjective*
the essence or important details, as in "Enough of this **blarney**, let's get down to the nitty-gritty." See also **crux.**

nonchalance (non-shuh-LONS) *noun*
an air of cool indifference; some people work hard to get this just right

nosey parker (NOH-zee PAR-ker) *noun*
a busybody; someone who sticks his or her nose in where it doesn't belong

oeuvre (UHVE) *noun*
an artist or writer's main body of work. The French phrase
hors d'oeuvre, which we pronounce "or-DERVE" and also
call appetizer, means outside of the main work, that is,
before or apart from the main course.

omnibus (OM-nee-bus) *noun*
a large passenger vehicle (bus); also an anthology of works
by an author

oodles (OO-duhlz) *noun*
lots and lots. See also **umpteen**.

oompah (OOM-pah) *noun*
the sound made by a tuba or similar instrument. Not to be
confused with Oompa-Loompas, the fictional pygmies in
Charlie and the Chocolate Factory.

WORDPLAY

An oxymoron is an expression or figure of speech that contains words
that would normally be contradictory, like "fine mess," "deafening
silence," and "quiet riot." The word *oxymoron* is itself an oxymoron
because it comes from the Greek words *oxo* (sharp) and *moros* (dull)!

is for

ornery (OR-ner-ee) *adjective*
difficult, irritable, stubborn, resistant to change. This word
developed as a contraction of the word *ordinary* (ordin'ry),
which in the early nineteenth century meant coarse or of
low quality. See also **cantankerous** and **contrariwise**.

ostentatious (oss-tin-TAY-shus) *adjective*
an obvious and showy display of wealth. People who make
ostentatious displays are called show-offs, and the word
swank is a noun that means ostentatious behavior.

outlandish
(out-LAND-ish) *adjective*
out of the ordinary, to
the point of being quite
strange. This word is also
a synonym for *foreign,*
which makes sense when
you break *outlandish* into
its three syllables.

parachute with panache

palsy-walsy (PAL-zee-WAL-zee) *adjective*
very friendly, usually in an annoying
way, as in "Well, you two have been very
palsy-walsy lately."

panache (puh-NASH) *noun*
an exaggerated or flowery style, as in "She signed her name
with little legibility but a lot of panache."

pantaloons (pant-uh-LOONZ) *noun*
loose-fitting trousers that finish above the ankle. During the
nineteenth century, pantaloons were tight-fitting trousers
secured by straps that passed under the foot; these made a
comeback in the 1980s as stirrup pants.

paraphernalia (pare-uh-fer-NALE-yuh) *noun*
your personal belongings—accessories, equipment,
anything that you carry around. See also **accoutrements**.

peccadillo (pek-uh-DIL-oh) *noun*
a very small wrongdoing, nothing worth getting your underwear in a twist about

pell-mell (pel-MEL) *adverb*
in a hasty or disorderly way, as in "I went running pell-mell
down the hill." Not to be confused with Pall Mall, which is a
famous street in London.

perambulate (per-AM-byoo-late) *verb*
to take a stroll or walk around. The British
word for baby stroller is *pram*, which is
a short version of *perambulator*.

persnickety (per-SNIK-uh-tee) *adjective*
overly concerned with small, often insignificant, details.
See also **fussbudget**.

piddling (PID-leeng) *adjective*
trifling, small, and inconsequential, as in a piddling amount
of Halloween candy

pizzazz (pih-ZAZ) *noun*
spice, excitement, glamour, vivacity, a splash of something
extra. Any word with four Zs in it has a lot of pizzazz . . .
see also **razzmatazz**.

plethora (PLEH-thuh-ruh) *noun*
an abundance of something, more than enough, as in a
plethora of Halloween candy

WORD PLAY

Has anyone ever told you to amscray? If so, they were speaking in Pig Latin, the
easiest secret code to learn. No one knows for sure how old Pig Latin is, but rumor
has it that Benjamin Franklin used a version of it in some of his publications.

potentate (POH-tin-tate) *noun*
a powerful king or other kind of ruler; someone with potent
or supreme power

privy (PRIH-vee) *adjective, noun*
As an adjective, this means sharing in the secret, as in
"I'm not privy to that information." But as a noun, this is
an old-timey word for a bathroom, aka an outhouse.

promenade (prah-mih-NADE or prah-mih-NOD) *noun, verb*
This is a place where you might take a nice, long, leisurely
stroll. But this is also a part of a square dance in which
couples move in a counterclockwise circle, so you'll want to
know this word if you ever become a square-dance caller:
"Swing your partner round and round, lift her up, set her
down. Do-si-do to and fro, jig to the left, and promenade
home."

pugilist (PYOO-juh-list) *noun*
someone who fights
professionally, such as
a boxer

purloin (per-LOYN) *verb*
to take something that doesn't belong to you. It's a fancier
way of saying "to steal."

Q
is for

quagmire (KWAG-my-er) *noun*
a mushy, marshy, swampy area, but also any kind of sticky situation or predicament

quahog (KOH-hog) *noun*
a thick-shelled clam

quandary (KWAHN-dree) *noun*
a state of doubt. People talk about "being in a quandary" when they have a difficult decision to make.

querulous (KWER-yoo-less) *adjective*
whiny and prone to complaining

quibble (KWIH-buhl) *verb*
to argue about trivial
details, as in "Let's not
quibble over who had it
first. It's mine now."

quixotic (kwik-SAH-tik) *adjective*
foolish, impractical. The word comes from the novel
Don Quixote, in which a farmer fancies himself a knight
and goes around attacking windmills. See also **capricious**.

quorum (KWOR-um) *noun*
a select group of people

WORD PLAY

The letter Q is worth 10 points in the game of Scrabble, and the
word quixotry could earn you as much as 365 points. Of course,
you would have to play it on triple-letter and triple-word squares
and you would nab a 50-point bonus for using all of your tiles.

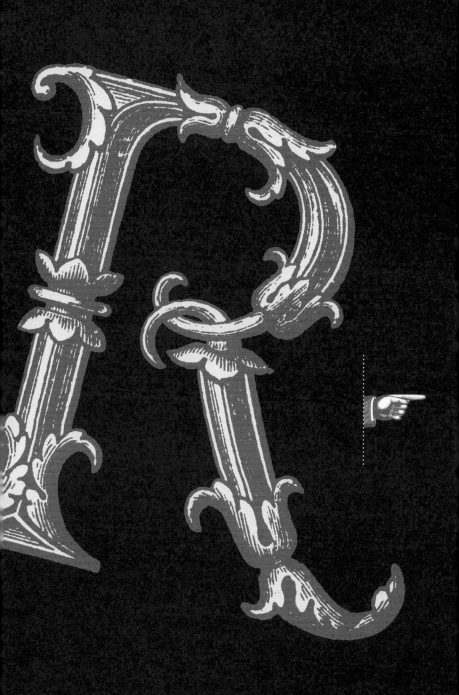

rabble-rouser (RA-buhl-row-zer) *noun*
a troublemaker, an instigator, someone who stirs up anger
in a group of people. (A rabble is a disorderly and confused
collection of things, such as a mob.)

raconteur (ra-kon-TER) *noun*
someone who is good at telling stories, who can "spin a good
yarn." This word is handiest when said in a sarcastic way, as
in "Well, aren't you *quite* the raconteur!"

ragamuffin (RA-guh-muh-fin) *noun*
a dirty and disheveled person, often a child. A ragamuffin is
also a relatively new breed of long-haired cat.

rapacious (ruh-PAY-shus) *adjective*
greedy and grasping

rickety rabbit

rapscallion (rap-SKAL-yun) *noun*
Originally spelled *rascallion*,
this is another word for a rascal.

razzmatazz (RAZ-muh-TAZ) *noun*
another way of saying "razzle dazzle,"
which is something complex, confusing, or gaudy

rigmarole (RIH-guh-muh-role) *noun*
an overly complex way of doing things

rogue (ROHG) *noun, adjective*
As a noun, this is a dishonest or unreliable person (see
also **scalawag**); as an adjective, it means dangerous or
uncontrollable, like a rogue elephant or a rogue wave.

rollick (RAH-lik) *verb*
to behave in a joyful way. Sometimes this word is used as an
adjective; you could say that you "had a rollicking good time"
at the party.

roughneck (RUF-nek) *adjective, noun*
a rough and tough person; a nickname for someone who
works on an oil rig

roundabout (ROWND-uh-bowt) *adjective*
the long and least direct way of doing something, as in
"We would have gotten here on time if *someone* hadn't
taken the roundabout way."

roustabout (ROWST-uh-bowt) *noun*
a person who works behind the scenes in a circus; a person
who loads and unloads ships; a nickname for someone who
works on an oil rig; or someone who stirs up trouble (see
also **rabble-rouser**)

R

is for

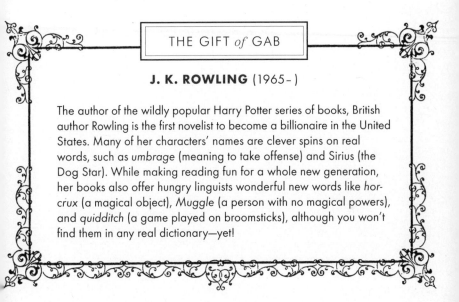

THE GIFT *of* GAB

J. K. ROWLING (1965–)

The author of the wildly popular Harry Potter series of books, British author Rowling is the first novelist to become a billionaire in the United States. Many of her characters' names are clever spins on real words, such as *umbrage* (meaning to take offense) and Sirius (the Dog Star). While making reading fun for a whole new generation, her books also offer hungry linguists wonderful new words like *horcrux* (a magical object), *Muggle* (a person with no magical powers), and *quidditch* (a game played on broomsticks), although you won't find them in any real dictionary—yet!

ruckus (RUK-us) *noun*
a big disturbance

ruffian (RUH-fee-yun) *noun*
an uncivilized person fond of a fight. It's another one of those words such as **rogue** that refers to a rough and unreliable person.

rumpus (RUM-pus) *noun*
a noisy commotion; rumpus rooms were created to keep the noisy commotion contained in one spot

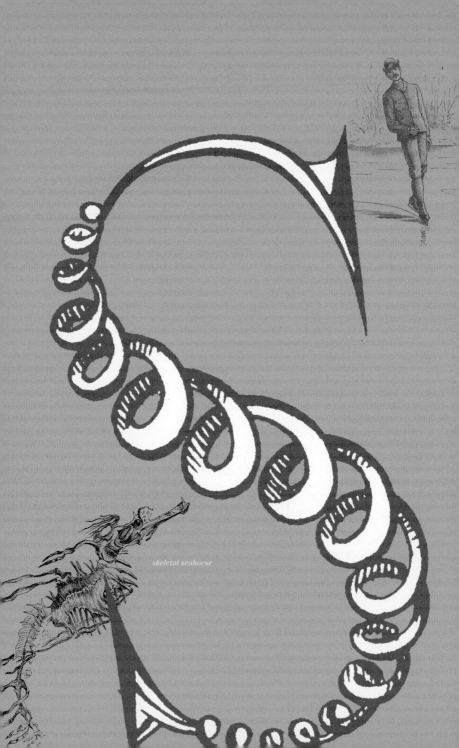

skeletal seahorse

saboteur (sa-buh-TERR) *noun*
someone who's guilty of sabotage (purposely messing
something up). It's a very enjoyable word to say, especially
when you stretch out the last syllable (in a snooty accent,
preferably) and yell, "Halt, you rascally saboteur!"

sarsaparilla (sass-puh-RILL-uh) *noun*
a flavored soda that is made with sassafras and tastes a lot
like root beer. It's not as popular as it was in the olden days,
but the next time you find yourself in an Old West saloon
(maybe on your way to the **haberdasher**), ask the barkeep
to pour you one.

savvy (SA-vee) *noun, adjective, verb*
As a noun, this means intelligence or know-how; as an
adjective, it means hip or wise; and as a verb, it means to
know or understand. Savvy?

savvy skaters

scalawag (SKA-luh-wag) *noun*
A cross between a **rogue** and a **ruffian**, this is yet another word for those darn wrongdoers in our midst. *Scalawag* was popularized as a term of contempt for a Southerner who collaborated with the Reconstruction governments after the American Civil War.

SCALAWAGS, CURMUDGEONS, AND OTHER ROGUES . . .

Ebenezer Scrooge	**Lord Voldemort**
Captain Hook	Wicked Witch of the West
Lex Luthor	**Darth Vader**
Snidely Whiplash	**The cantankerous** old coot living in the mansion on the hill
Dick Dastardly	

scofflaw (SKAH-flah) *noun*
someone who breaks the law in a deliberate way—someone who "scoffs at the law"

scrimshaw (SKRIM-shaw) *noun*
carvings made from whale bones. A person who creates scrimshaw is a scrimshander.

scurvy (SKER-vee) *adjective, noun*
As an adjective, this means despicable, as in "You'll pay for that, you scurvy dog!" As a noun, it is a disease caused by lack of vitamin C, common among sailors who went on long voyages without fresh fruits and vegetables. ("Argh, matey, don't want to get the scurvy. Best eat me limes.")

serendipity (sare-en-DIP-ih-tee) *noun*
the phenomenon of accidentally encountering or receiving something good that you weren't looking for. *The Three Princes of Serendip* is a Persian fairy tale in which the main characters encounter many happy accidents.

shenanigans
(sheh-NA-nih-gunz) *noun*
devious tricks or mischievous behavior. Although it is possible to engage in one shenanigan, there's more of an impact if you work up a bunch of them. See also **tomfoolery**.

shindig (SHIN-dig) *noun*
a party. It has a bit of a 1960s feel, especially if you say,
"This is a swingin' shindig, man!"

sidewinder (SIDE-wine-der) *noun*
a heavy blow or punch that swings in from the side.
A sidewinder is also a small rattlesnake that slithers
in S-shaped curves. See also **haymaker**.

skedaddle (skih-DA-duhl) *verb*
to make a break for it or get going while the going's good

skinflint (SKIN-flint) *noun*
a mean and miserly person who hates spending money;
penny-pincher

skulk (SKUHLK) *verb*
to move about in a stealthy manner. You should probably
be suspicious of anyone who skulks.

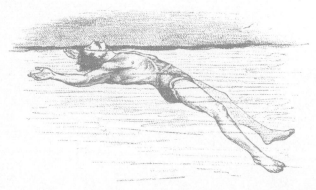

stargazing swimmer

PLAYING WITH WORDS

····· Try working these expressions into your repertoire:

peachy keen *mighty fine*

23-skiddo *same as "Let's get out of here," just like **skedaddle***

tail over teakettle *same as "head over heels"*

a horse of a different color *something else entirely different*

the cat's meow *fantastic! ("The cat's pajamas" and "the bee's knees" mean the same thing.)*

olly olly oxen free! *the classic "all safe" call from the game Hide and Seek*

knee high to a grasshopper *not very tall*

cruisin' for a bruisin' *just asking for trouble*

over the moon *feeling really great*

by hook or by crook *by any means necessary*

skullduggery (skuhl-DUG-er-ee) *noun*
underhanded and sneaky behavior, as in "It seems to me
there is some skullduggery afoot here, and I intend to get
to the bottom of it."

smattering (SMA-ter-eeng) *noun*
a small amount. See also **piddling**.

smithereens (smith-er-EENZ) *noun*
small pieces, especially the small pieces left after something
has been blown up

snollygoster (SNAH-lee-gost-er) *noun*
a shrewd or crooked person; a swindler. (Disappearing
word alert! This word has been removed from some newer
dictionaries.)

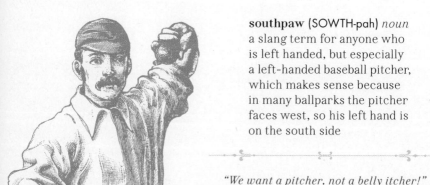

southpaw (SOWTH-pah) *noun*
a slang term for anyone who
is left handed, but especially
a left-handed baseball pitcher,
which makes sense because
in many ballparks the pitcher
faces west, so his left hand is
on the south side

"We want a pitcher, not a belly itcher!"

sPindLe-shaNked

(SPIN-duhl-shankt) *adjective*
having long, skinny legs; also
known as "spider-shanked."
See also **longshanks**.

squeamish
(SKWEE-mish) *adjective*
easily nauseated (queasy)
or easily offended

squeezebox
(SKWEEZ-boks) *noun*
a slang term for any musical
instrument that's shaped like a
box and produces a tune when
it's squeezed together,
such as an accordion

sneering swine

subterfuge (SUB-ter-fyooj) *noun*
a sneaky strategy or underhanded action that some sly and **dastardly** person might use in order to get what he or she wants

succotash (SUK-uh-tash) *noun*
a dish of lima beans and corn kernels. "Sufferin' succotash!" is the favorite exclamation of Sylvester the cat.

surly (SER-lee) *adjective*
grumpy, crabby, or even menacing, as in "Looks like someone woke up on the surly side of the bed."

swagger (SWAG-er) *verb*
to walk around in an overly confident manner

WORD PLAY

A spoonerism is the swapping of sounds in words, whether as a slip of the tongue or as a purposeful play on words. It is named after William Spooner, a nineteenth-century clergyman who supposedly told a new groom, "It is kisstomary to cuss the bride."

SWASHBUCKLER (SWOSH-buk-ler) *noun*

a daring and dashing pirate, soldier, or adventurer who is usually good with a sword, such as Robin Hood or Zorro. But in the sixteenth century, a swashbuckler was a loud-mouthed **swaggering** bully.

swizzle (SWIH-zuhl) *noun, verb*

an alcoholic drink or cocktail. A swizzle stick is the utensil used to stir alcoholic drinks. But as a verb, *swizzle* means to drink greedily, like *guzzle* or *chug*, so if you swizzled a swizzle, you'd make yourself pretty sick.

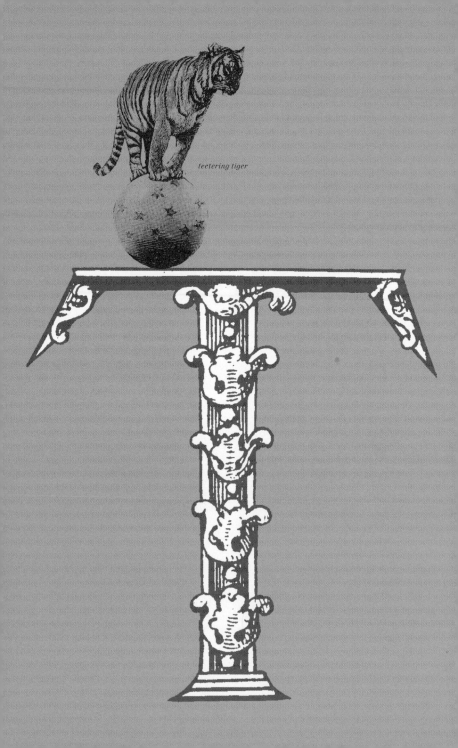

teetering tiger

tallyho! (ta-lee-HOH) *interjection*
a fox-hunting cry shouted when the fox is spotted

tchotchke (CHOCH-kee) *noun*
a souvenir or trinket. See also
knickknack.

teetotaler (TEE-TOH-tuhl-er) *noun*
someone who practices teetotalism, which is the refusal to
drink any alcohol. The word *teetotal* was invented as a way of
emphasizing the *T* in *total*.

tenterhooks (TEN-ter-huhks) *noun*
sharp hooks used to fasten clothing; to be "on tenterhooks"
means to be anxious about something

tiddlywinks (TID-lee-weenks) *noun*
a game of skill and aim played with small counters.
The object is to use one of the counters to snap the edge
of another, and so send it flying into a dish or cup.

is for

tintinnabulation (tin-tih-nab-yoo-LAY-shun) *noun*
the jingling sound that bells make

tomfoolery (tom-FOO-ler-ee) *noun*
silly behavior. See also **shenanigans**.

topsy-turvy (TOP-see-TER-vee) *adjective, adverb*
in complete confusion or, to put it another way, upside down

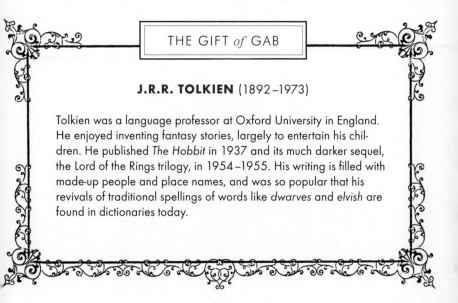

THE GIFT *of* GAB

J.R.R. TOLKIEN (1892–1973)

Tolkien was a language professor at Oxford University in England. He enjoyed inventing fantasy stories, largely to entertain his children. He published *The Hobbit* in 1937 and its much darker sequel, the Lord of the Rings trilogy, in 1954–1955. His writing is filled with made-up people and place names, and was so popular that his revivals of traditional spellings of words like *dwarves* and *elvish* are found in dictionaries today.

troubadour (TROO-buh-dor) *noun*
a fancy word for a folk singer. Troubadours were the poet-musicians who traveled the countryside entertaining royalty during the Middle Ages.

truncate (TRUN-kate) *verb*
to shorten by removing or cutting something off

turncoat (TERN-kote) *noun*
a traitor, someone who crosses over to the other side; it comes from the idea of turning your coat inside out to pass yourself off as one of the enemy

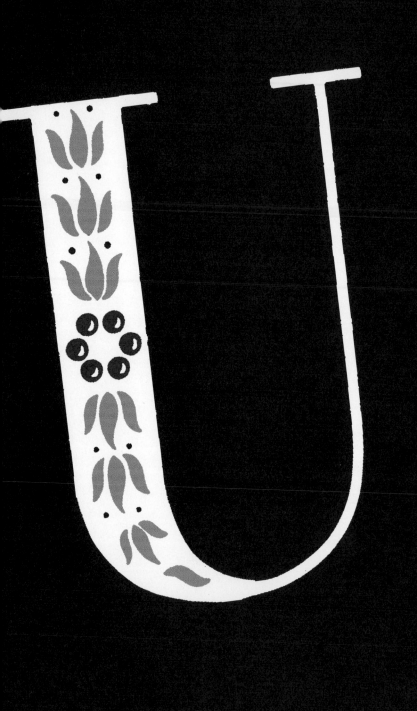

umpteen (UM-teen) *adjective*
a way to say "many" when you don't know the exact
number. You've probably heard your mother use this
word umpteen times. See also **oodles**.

underbelly (UN-der-beh-lee) *noun*
the hidden underside of something. The underbelly of
a city is the less wholesome part of town.

undercarriage (UN-der-kare-ij) *noun*
the underside of a car or airplane

underling (UN-der-leeng) *noun*
somebody who gets bossed around by somebody else

undulation (un-joo-LAY-shun) *noun*
a steady up-and-down or to-and-fro motion; sometimes used as a fancy word for speed bumps

*Did you know that "Thank-you-ma'am"
is a slang expression for a bump or dip in the road?
It makes sense because hitting a bump causes you
to nod your head like a gentleman nods to a lady.*

uppity (UH-pih-tee) *adjective*
having an air of superiority

usurp (yoo-SERP) *verb*
to take somebody else's place, sometimes by force and always without having the right to do so, as in "I have no idea how it happened, but that rascal has usurped my position as the most popular girl in school!"

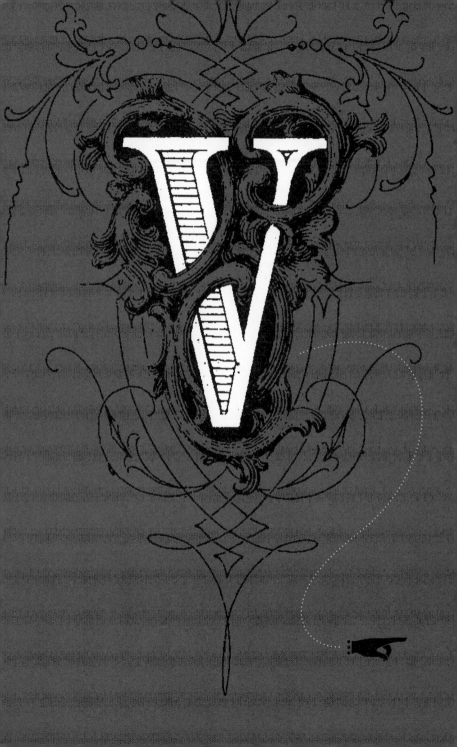

V

is for

velocipede (vuh-LAH-sih-peed) *noun*
a vehicle with three wheels that was an early version of
the bicycle; and then there was the dandy-horse, which
had two wheels but no pedals

verisimilitude (vare-ih-sih-MIL-ih-tood) *noun*
the appearance of truth or reality, which is good to
have, especially when you're not actually telling the
truth or living in reality

vexation (vek-SAY-shun) *noun*
all kinds of annoyance, exasperation, botheration, and
peevishness

vigilante (vih-jih-LAN-tee) *noun*
someone who takes the law into their own hands, who
seeks to punish criminals or set things right on their own.
Although in real life vigilantism can lead to more trouble,
we usually root for the vigilantes in movies and books.

vignette (vin-YET) *noun*
a short but descriptive passage in a book or scene
in a movie

vim and verve (VIM and VERV) *noun*
If you've got vim and verve, you got spunk, energy, and
enthusiasm. See also **chutzpah**, **gumption**, and **moxie**.

viscosity (vis-CAH-sih-tee) *noun*
the level of goopiness in a substance that determines how
fast it will flow; molasses and other sticky substances have a
high level of viscosity

vomitory (VAH-mih-tor-ee) *noun*
the passageway running between rows of seats that specta-
tors use to enter or exit a stadium; it comes from the Latin
verb *vomere*, meaning to eject or spew forth

very valuable Victorian vehicle

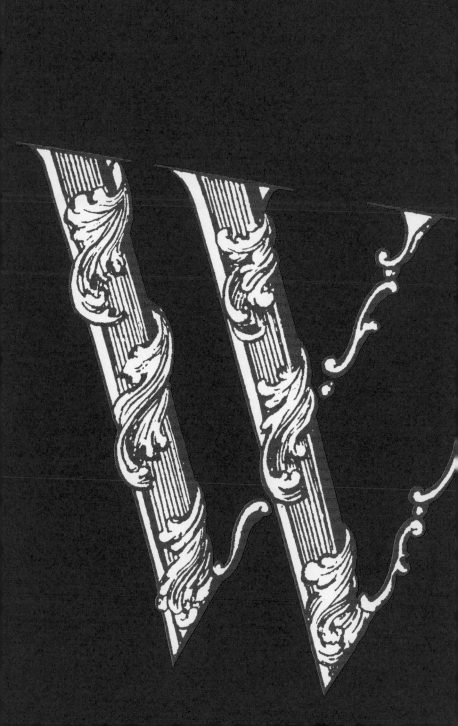

walleyed (WOLL-ide) *adjective*
when you're so shocked or excited
that your eyes bug out like a fish's

wallop (WOLL-up) *verb*
to hit or thump with force. It's simply impossible to wallop
someone gently. As an interjection, *walloping* means
fantastic or exceptionally great.

whatchamacallit (WUH-chuh-muh-coll-it) *noun*
an object whose name you just can't remember. You
know, a thingy, a thingamajig, a whatsit. That's right—
a whatchamacallit!

wherewithal (WARE-with-oll) *noun*
the necessary means; the stuff needed to do something,
as in "I wanted to open my own **gumshoe** business, but
I lacked the wherewithal."

whippersnapper (WIP-er-snap-er) *noun*
a young person who is cheeky and maybe a little sassy.
Whippersnappers usually have a lot of **chutzpah** and
have a tendency to **irk** people, especially **curmudgeons**.

whirligig (WER-lee-gig) *noun*
something that spins around and around,
like a top or a merry-go-round

whirling dervish (WER-leeng DER-vish) *noun*
another something that spins around and around,
except this is a person who spins around as part of
a ritual dance

W

is for

will-o'-the-wisp (wih-loh-thuh-WISP) *noun*
Besides being a villain in the Superman comic books and a
monster in the Dungeons and Dragons game, a will-o'-the-
wisp is a legendary ghostly, flickering light seen at night
over bogs. It is also known as fool's fire and so also refers to
a foolish goal.

willy-nilly (WIH-lee-NIH-lee) *adjective*
haphazard or sloppy, as in "They were thrown together all
willy-nilly like." It comes from the old expression "will ye,
nill ye."

wisenheimer (WY-zen-hy-mer) *noun*
a smart aleck or wise guy, someone who is a bit too clever
for his own good

wishy-washy (WIH-shee-wah-shee) *adjective*
weak and unsatisfying; lacking character or substance

woebegone (WOH-beh-gon) *adjective*
feeling a lot of woe, so much woe
that you go around sighing and
mumbling, "Woe is me."

wonky (WON-kee) *adjective*
shaky or unsteady. See also **awry**.

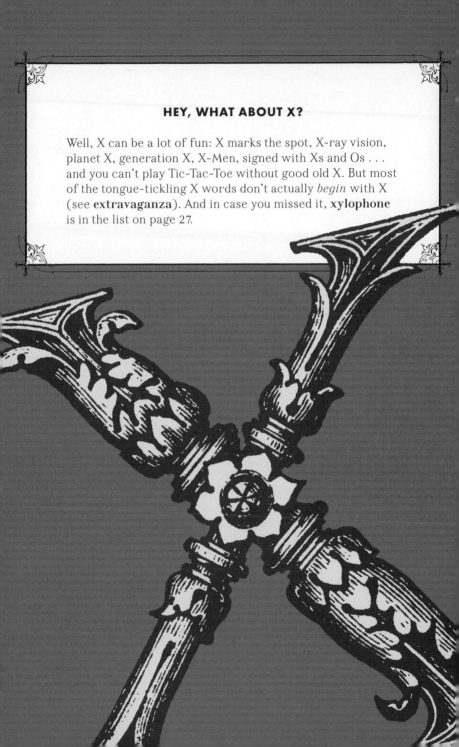

HEY, WHAT ABOUT X?

Well, X can be a lot of fun: X marks the spot, X-ray vision, planet X, generation X, X-Men, signed with Xs and Os . . . and you can't play Tic-Tac-Toe without good old X. But most of the tongue-tickling X words don't actually *begin* with X (see **extravaganza**). And in case you missed it, **xylophone** is in the list on page 27.

Y

is for

yawp (YAWP) *verb*
to squawk or to complain, in the sense that
the squeaky wheel gets the grease

"I sound my barbaric yawp over the roofs of the world."
— *Walt Whitman*

yellow-bellied (YEH-loh-beh-leed) *adjective*
a description of many types of birds,
this is also slang for weak and easily
frightened. See also **lily-livered**.

yeoman (YOH-mun) *noun*
someone who does a great job
or performs a really useful service

yonder (YON-der) *adjective, adverb*
you know: somewhere up ahead, over there,
in the distance but not too far away

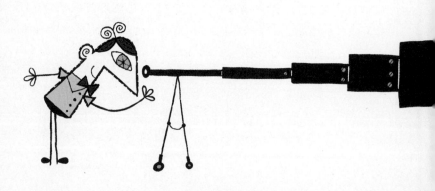

Z

is for

Zamboni (zam-BOH-nee) *noun*
a trucklike machine used to
smooth the surface of ice
rinks. *Zamboni* is capitalized
because it is a trademark—
the machine was invented
by Frank J. Zamboni in 1949
—although all brands of ice-
resurfacing machines are
referred to by this name.

zeitgeist (ZITE-giste) *noun*
the general spirit of an era.
For example, the zeitgeist of
the 1920s—also known
as the Roaring Twenties
—was fun and frivolity;
the zeitgeist of the 1930s
was more serious because
of the hardships of the Great
Depression.

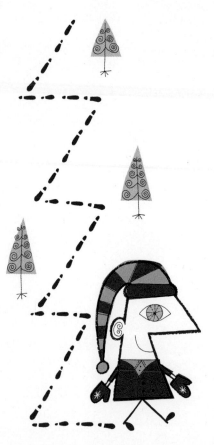

zigzag (ZIG-zag) *adjective, adverb, noun, verb*
cutting across from side to side. If you need to waste a
few hours, you could measure the zigzaggedness of the
zippers on all your pants.

zoetrope (ZOH-eh-trope) *noun*
a cylindrical device that spins a sequence of images to give
the illusion of motion, like a mini-movie

Zulu (ZOO-loo) *noun*
a South African ethnic group, and also the last letter of the
aviation alphabet (the first letter is alpha)

zydeco (ZY-deh-koh) *noun*
music from Southern Louisiana. It's a **jambalaya** of French,
Caribbean, and blues influences.

THE ——————————— END!

The answer is . . .

the letter

Remember the **conundrum** *from page 23?*

ZEITGEIST

kvun

tiddlywinks

roustabout

diabolical   barnstormer   *persnickety*   swashbuckler

{{{ .... **HANKERING** *for* **more?** }

There are many more words worth wrapping your tongue
around, but they couldn't all be squished into the pages of
this book. But don't let that stop you from playing with your
words! Start your own list and add to it whenever you hear
a word that makes you smile or think to yourself, "Ooh,
good word." You can even try inventing your own quirky
words. Hey, if Shakespeare could do it, why can't you?

tintinnabulation

oompah   *extemporaneous*   topsy-turvy

GALUMPH   ∽   DOPPELGÄNGER